In bed

ELEPHANT

P. H. SCOTT

THE SALTIRE SOCIETY
1985

ISBN 0 85411 003 8

British Library Cataloguing in Publication Data

Designed and produced by
Fianach Lawry Associates/Ruari McLean
Printed by
W. M. Bett Ltd, Tillicoultry

Contents

I. *The Three Hundred Years' War*

It was Pierre Trudeau, I believe, who said that for Canada to share a continent with the United States was like a man having to share a bed with an elephant. It is an experience which can be dangerous or very uncomfortable and lead to pressures which are difficult to avoid or resist. The elephant can use its sheer bulk and weight to flatten resistance altogether. This can happen even by accident without any malicious intention. If there is a conflict of interests or of tastes, weight is liable to predominate. This sort of experience is common whenever a country has a neighbour much larger and wealthier than itself. The world is full of examples, but one which has a longer history than most, some 700 years at least, is the case of Scotland and England. I should like to look at this example, which affects almost every aspect of our lives. It is a long and continuing story and, to understand it at all, it is necessary to begin with a little history.

The relationship between Scotland and England is the oldest of its kind in Europe, because they were the first countries to consolidate within very much the same borders as still exist. You could trace this border back to the time of the Roman Empire because it closely coincides with Hadrian's Wall. At all events, by the end of the thirteenth century both Scotland and England were relatively consolidated and prosperous states, living in relative peace and harmony with one another. This was an era which came to an abrupt end with the accidental death of King Alexander III of Scotland in 1286. The oldest surviving Scottish poem looks back to his reign as a lost Golden Age, because Edward I of England seized the opportunity of the disputed succession to attempt to take over Scotland, first by diplomatic manipulation and then, when that failed, by force. It was a pattern that was to be repeated frequently for the next 300 years, with the slaughter and destruction renewed in each attack.

The destructive effects of this prolonged attempt to conquer or subvert Scotland are beyond calculation; it was the longest war in European history. English historians, to their credit, have written some of the strongest condemnations of it. Henry Thomas Buckle, for example:

> "The darling object of the English, was to subjugate the Scotch; and if anything could increase the disgrace of so base an enterprise, it would have been that, having undertaken it, they ignominiously failed."[1]

Or James Anthony Froude:

> "The English hated Scotland because Scotland had successfully defied them: the Scots hated England as an enemy on the watch to make them slaves. The hereditary hostility strengthened with time, and each generation added fresh injuries to the accumulation of bitterness."[2]

It was the misfortune of Scotland to have on her border a country which was not only larger, and therefore more powerful, but which was, for centuries, particularly aggressive and expansionist. Scotland, Wales, Ireland and France were all exposed to repeated English efforts to subjugate them, with varying degrees of success. Every country within reach was fair game. Scotland had the further misfortune that the richest part of the country in the south was the most exposed to English attack and was frequently laid waste.

The national consciousness of Scotland, tempered in the crucible of this long struggle, found early expression in three notable documents. The first of these, the *Declaration of Arbroath of* 1320, was a diplomatic despatch in Latin. It was outstanding among such documents for its eloquence and passion but also for the startling originality, at such an early date, of its political ideas. The orthodox view among modern historians is that the idea of national self-determination evolved at about the time of the French Revolution with Rousseau's doctrine that sovereignty resides in the people and not the ruler. About 400 years before Rousseau, the same fundamental philosophy is expressed clearly and powerfully in this Declaration. Scotland is the oldest nation in Europe because it was the first to evolve two related ideas: that the distinctiveness of a national community is worth defending for its own sake, and that rulers exist to serve the community and not the reverse. There is a paragraph in the Declaration where these two ideas are combined. The previous passage refers to the appointment of Robert as King "with the due consent and assent of us all". It then continues:

> "Yet if he should give up what he has begun, and agree to make us or our kingdom subject to the King of England or the English, we should exert ourselves at once to drive him out as our enemy and a subverter of his own rights and ours, and make some other man who was well able to defend us our King; for, as long as but a hundred of us remain alive, never will we on any conditions be brought under English rule. It is in truth not for glory, nor riches, nor honours that we are fighting, but for freedom — for that alone, which no honest man gives up but with life itself."[3]

The constitutional principles of the Declaration of Arbroath have never ceased to strike echoes in Scotland. Let me give only one example. In his novel, *Ringan Gilhaize*, John Galt is concerned to justify the resort by the Covenanters to "the divine right of resistance" against established authority. He recalls the Declaration in support and, to make sure that the reader does not miss the point, prints the whole text as an appendix. Scottish constitutional theory has always tended to reject the notions that sovereignty resided with a King or with Parliament or with any institution other than the whole community. It follows from this that there is a manifest right to resist injustice from whatever source it comes. Another implication is the egalitarian view that all men have equal rights. This is another assumption which from these early times has strongly influenced Scottish attitudes to politics and religion.

The other two documents which emerged from the struggle for independence are works of a very different character from the Declaration, but they are imbued with the same spirit, the two long narrative or epic poems, Barbour's *Brus* and Hary's *Wallace*. They are two of the earliest surviving works of Scottish literature. So it is a literature which began with the celebration of the two national heroes of the War of Independence and with the assertion and elaboration of the ideas of the *Declaration of Arbroath*. The two poems have had a long-continuing influence, directly and indirectly. Until about the end of the eighteenth century, versions of them were among the most widely read books in Scotland. They in turn influenced other writers who continued to be read long after Barbour and Hary themselves had been relegated to the specialists. Robert Burns, for example, in his famous autobiographical letter to John Moore said: "the story of Wallace poured a Scottish prejudice in my veins which will boil along there till the flood-gates of life shut in eternal rest."[4] Many other people have said much the same. It is by such means as these that the epic Scottish struggle for independence has passed into legend or folk memory and helped to shape instinctive attitudes and responses.

One of the consequences of the long war of resistance against England was that Scotland was encouraged to seek markets, allies and cultural and intellectual exchange with continental Europe. For centuries, Scottish merchants, soldiers and scholars travelled everywhere, from Scandinavia to Italy, from Portugal to Russia. Many established themselves in country after country as generals, ambassadors, architects or professors. The contribution which many of these men made to the development of other countries in Europe is very remarkable. Take, for example, James Keith, exiled from Scotland by his Jacobitism. In Russia, he became a general at the age of 32, then Ambassador to Sweden and Governor of the Ukraine. He left the Russian service to become the right-hand man and Field Marshal of Frederick the Great. His brother, George, Earl Marischall of Scotland, was the Prussian Ambassador to Spain, Governor of Neuchatel and the only man to win the unqualified approval of Rousseau. Patrick Gordon, another native of Buchan, also became a Russian General and he was a key figure in the transformation of Russia under Peter the Great. After the Czar himself, John Hill Burton wrote, "it may be questioned if any other man did so much for the early consolidation of the Russian empire."[5] John Law of Lauriston shaped French financial policy and founded the Bank of France. George Buchanan, who wrote in Latin (one of the four languages of Scottish literature) was regarded as the leading poet in Europe, "poetarum nostri saeculi facile princeps." He was not only Principal of St Leonard's College in St Andrews, but at various times an intellectual force in the universities of Paris, Bordeaux and Coimbra in Portugal. These are only a few random examples from different countries and periods of the intimate Scottish relationship with Europe. Above all we had a close alliance with France for over 300 years, so close that the two countries exchanged citizenship and Scots formed the guard of the French Kings. We were actively and consciously European centuries before the EEC.

This Scottish involvement with the rest of Europe was so different from the much more insular and self-sufficient attitude of England that it alone accounts for many of the radical differences between the Scottish and English traditions. The

Scottish interchange with other countries in Europe brought foreign influence at its most stimulating and beneficial. It was diverse and accepted on its merits, not monolithic and imposed; it was quite different from suffocation by elephantine weight. Every aspect of life in Scotland from music and dance to architecture and law was affected by this European influence. In particular, the universities from the fifteenth century onwards developed in close touch with intellectual movements in the rest of Europe. Scottish scholars went, as a matter of course, to study and teach in the universities of France, Italy, Germany and the Low Countries. Many of them brought back new ideas to Scotland. Dugald Stewart, the first historian of the Scottish Enlightenment, had no doubt that its origins were to be found, at least partly, in this "constant influx of information and of liberality from abroad"[6] during the previous centuries. The Enlightenment was the culmination of a long process, not a sudden and mysterious apparition.

In spite of the constant devastation and wastage of the long war with England, the achievements of the medieval Scottish kingdom were considerable. They reached their highest point towards the end of the fifteenth century during the reign of James IV, a true Renaissance prince. It was the age of Henryson, Dunbar and Douglas, whose poetry was among the most impressive written in Europe in that century. Their language was Middle Scots, a rich and expressive tongue, used for all purposes and at all social levels. It was an age also of intellectual and artistic innovation in many diverse directions and of active involvement in European diplomacy. The demands of the French alliance led to the campaign which ended disastrously at the Battle of Flodden in 1513. So ended, abruptly, the bright hopes of the fifteenth-century Renaissance. Indeed it is possible that Scotland never fully recovered from that disaster. It was, wrote Francis Jeffrey, "the day that broke for ever the pride and splendour of the country."[7] In the present century, the film director John Grierson said: "We were driven into the wilderness of national poverty at Flodden by the English and the English have never let us out of it to this day."[8]

The sorry record of destruction continued long after Flodden. In 1544, for example, Henry VIII sent the English fleet under the Earl of Hertford to sack and burn Leith, Edinburgh, Holyrood and all the towns and villages between them and Dunbar. In the following year, the same Earl of Hertford crossed the Border by land and destroyed 5 market towns, 243 villages, 16 fortified places, hundreds of churches and the Abbeys of Kelso, Melrose, Dryburgh and Roxburgh. The ruins of these Abbeys remain to this day, giving us some idea of how much was lost. But Henry VIII's intervention in Scotland was not confined to marauding armies. Like other English rulers before and since, he used both the stick and the carrot, or, to be more precise, the sword and the bribe. He continued the traditional English policy of seeking out disaffected, greedy or ambitious Scots who could be bribed to serve English interests. There was often, therefore, a faction in Scotland who were secretly in the pay of England. This became a particularly tempting policy to England at the time of the Reformation when the spread of the new religious ideas offered the prospect of breaking Scotland's historical alliance with France. Then, as later, it was not easy to unravel the complex interplay of self-interest and ideological conviction.

II. *From the Reformation to the Enlightenment*

The Reformation led to a fundamental change in Scotland's international alliances and in the relationship with England. To Protestant Scotland the continuation of the alliance with

Catholic France became untenable. For the first time in more than 300 years, an element of mutual interest affected relations between England and Scotland and pressure towards co-operation instead of conflict began to be felt. So drastic a change did not come easily, but only after some two centuries or travail which culminated with the defeat of the Jacobites at Culloden in 1746. The sixteenth century, when this process began, was a time of quite extraordinary self-confidence in England, which was rationalised and encouraged by theological writers like John Foxe and John Aylmer. They interpreted the Book of Revelation to prove, to their own satisfaction, that Elizabeth was a latter-day Constantine, destined as a Godly Prince to defeat the Anti-Christ and save and lead the world. Aylmer even proclaimed that "God is English". Scottish reformers taking refuge in England, and in particular John Knox, came under the influence of these curious ideas, in spite of the destruction of what passed as argument by Napier of Merchiston. The acceptance by the Kirk in Scotland of the Authorised Version of the Bible in 1611 reflected a new attitude to England. To generations of Scots it carried the implication that whether or not God was English, he certainly spoke in English, and that it was the proper tongue for serious and weighty matters. Nothing could have done more to undermine the status of the Scots language at the time when it was beginning to evolve a prose to match its high achievement in verse.

In recent years, the Scottish Reformation has, on the whole, had a bad press, mainly because of its tendency to regard music, dance and the drama as frivolous distractions from the serious matter of man's relations with God. On the other hand, the Kirk has been a beneficial force in more than one direction. It embodies the Scottish egalitarian instinct and distrust of ranks and hierarchy in its representative structure of Kirk Sessions, Presbyteries, Synods and General Assembly. This was the first attempt in these islands to create democratic representation, open to all classes of the community, some 300 years before it was attempted in Parliament. Secondly, from the sixteenth century onwards, it placed high value on education and set about the task of establishing a free school in every parish. By the end of the following century, this policy had been so successful that the great historian T. B. Macaulay believed that it had made the common people in Scotland the most intelligent in Europe. "Scotland made such progress", he wrote "in all that constitutes civilisation, as the old world had never seen equalled, and as even the new world has scarcely seen surpassed. . . . This wonderful change is to be attributed, not indeed solely, but principally, to the national system of education."[9]

From its beginning, Calvinism has been an intellectual religion, elaborating its doctrines by a process of rigorous logic. This approach was followed not only by the theological writers but by every service in the Kirk. The emphasis was on a closely-argued sermon, which the congregation were expected both to follow and to subject to a critical analysis. In his novel *Rob Roy*, Walter Scott describes such a service in Glasgow Cathedral and he concludes:

> "The Scotch, it is well known, are more remarkable for the exercise of their intellectual powers, than for the keeness of their feelings; they are, therefore, more moved by logic than by rhetoric, and more attracted by acute and argumentative reasoning on doctrinal points, than influenced by the enthusiastic appeals to the heart and to the passions, by which popular preachers in other countries win the favour of their hearers."[10]

Whether the Kirk created or responded to this national addiction to metaphysical speculation and logical argument, the fact is that for a long period most of the population were exposed to this sort of intellectual exercise every Sunday of their lives.

The parish schools produced a high level of literacy, probably higher than any other country in Europe for about 300 years. The universities were in touch with the movements of European thought. The whole people were trained in "acute and argumentative reasoning" by the services of the Kirk. All these influences together prepared the way for the intellectual and artistic explosion of the eighteenth century. As John MacQueen has said, "The Scottish Enlightenment was the natural, almost the inevitable, outcome of several centuries of Scottish and European intellectual history."[11]

The change which the Reformation brought to the relationship with England was reinforced by a dynastic accident, the succession of a Scottish King, James VI, to the English throne in 1603. This was a consequence of the marriage of the daughter of Henry VII of England to James IV of Scotland. When it was under discussion in the English Court, some of Henry's advisers pointed to the risk that it might bring England under the rule of a Scottish prince. Henry told them not to worry. If that happened, it would mean the accession, not of England to Scotland, but of Scotland to England, since "the greater would always draw the less, as England had drawn Normandy under her sway."[12] He was right. The transfer of the Royal Court to London deprived Scotland at a stroke of the control of the Executive, of state appointments and of the conduct of foreign policy. Royal patronage of the arts disappeared with the King. Scots was no longer the language of a royal Court and inevitably began to lose the status of a national speech. In the words of Hume Brown, Scotland had become "a severed and a withered branch and her people knew it."

By the beginning of the eighteenth century, this position had become intolerable. The Monarch was still much more than a constitutional myth, and in fact the effective head of executive government. Scotland was nominally independent, but was subject to a Monarch who was under the strong influence of English ministers. Matters came to a head over the Darien Scheme, approved by William as King of Scotland, but undermined by him as King of England. The Scottish Parliament of 1703, largely under the inspiration of Andrew Fletcher of Saltoun, decided that it must either free policy and its execution from royal control or choose a separate successor to the throne of Scotland. The English response was to press for an incorporating union which would absorb the Scottish Parliament in the same way as the Scottish monarchy had been absorbed. This was achieved in 1707, in defiance of the wishes of the people of Scotland at large, by a mixture of bribery, propaganda and military intimidation.[13]

The Jacobite risings were in part an expression of hostility to the Union, but the issue was not simple and clear-cut. Part of the price which England had been prepared to pay for the Union was the acceptance, and indeed guarantee, of the Presbyterian Kirk in Scotland. A restoration of the Stuarts implied the revival of the French alliance and a threat to Presbyterianism. This was a dilemma which meant a painful choice between unpalatable alternatives. Scots might opt, in all conscience, for either side. There were therefore Scots in Cumberland's army at Culloden and some were involved in the barbarous oppression which he carried out in the Highlands after the battle. This, the first exercise of English power in Scotland after the Union, was an act of genocide, the deliberate suppression of a people, a way of life, a culture and a language.

From the earliest times, Scotland has been a multi-racial and a multilingual community. We have literatures in four languages, Gaelic, Latin, Scots and English. At the time of Culloden, Gaelic was spoken in more than half of the country and by about a third of the people. As a direct consequence of the policies imposed after Culloden, which made the Clearances possible, most of the Highlands are now largely uninhabited, and Gaelic has been driven to its last stronghold in the Western Isles. Perthshire, for instance, had a rich oral literature in poetry and story. With the loss of the language, the curtain falls and only scraps of the literature remain. In the words which Tacitus attributed to Galgacus, "They made a desert and they called it peace."

It was against this discouraging background that occurred the great effloresence of the Scottish eighteenth century, a period of achievement in literature, science and the arts, for which you can find a parallel in a small country only in Periclean Athens or Renaissance Florence. Certainly, it was the culmination of a long process; so rich a growth can only spring from deep roots. Perhaps also, in a paradoxical way, the immediate political circumstances were a spur to effort. The humiliation of 1707 had threatened the extinction of Scotland. Now the intellect and the arts were being called in evidence to show that Scotland was not to be ignored. One aspect of this was a determination to find new life in the old literary roots. This was explicit in the anthologies of the older poetry, such as John Watson's *Choice Collection* of 1706 and Allan Ramsay's *The Ever Green* of 1724, which were among the first signs of revival. Like MacDiarmid in the present century, they went back to Dunbar as a preparation for a new advance. Burns collected songs and Scott the ballads in the same spirit of resistance to cultural assimilation. Ramsay, Fergusson and Burns wrote poetry in Scots with this conscious purpose, and all three strongly condemned the Union. Both Scott and Galt were anxious to record a Scottish way of life that was being eroded under pressure, and they used Scots as a necessary part of this. At the same time, and in the same spirit, there was a rich flowering of Gaelic poetry in the work of Alasdair Mac Mhaigstir Alasdair, Donnchadh Ban, Rob Donn and Uilleam Ros.

On the other hand, the philosophers, historians, econo-mists and sociologists, Hume, Robertson, Smith, Adam Ferguson and the others, took pains to write in English but it was not the language which they spoke. An English visitor, Edward Topham, said of them: "They appear to me, from their conversation, to write English as a foreign tongue; their mode of talking, phrase and expression, but little resembling the language of their works."[14] They wrote English partly for the same reason that George Buchanan wrote Latin, to reach a wider audience. Also, they were faced with a difficult choice. As Ramsay of Ochtertyre explained it at the time, the events of the seventeenth century had frustrated the development of a Scots prose. In the following century, the literati had either to undertake what Ramsay called the "Herculean labour" of creating a prose suitable for their purposes or the only slightly less difficult task of learning to write English. "In this generous but unpromising attempt our countrymen at length succeeded, to the conviction of all the world".[15] To some extent, Ramsay was looking for an excuse. The need to find a workable prose does not explain the neurotic anxiety with which the literati excised every Scots word or turn of phrase and which provoked the old joke that Hume died confessing not his sins but his Scotticisms.

There was a parallel in the content of their writing. They were preoccupied with the evolution of human society. This was forced on their attention because they were living in Scotland at a time of particularly rapid and violent change, following the loss of independence, the destruction of High-land society after the '45 and the beginning of the industrial revolution. But if their ideas evolved from their Scottish experience, there is remarkably little sign of it in their writing. Take the case of Adam Ferguson. He was a Gaelic-speaking Highlander, born in Logierait in Perthshire in 1724, and he spent nine years as chaplain to the Highland regiment, the Black Watch, immediately after Culloden. In one of his surviving letters, he makes it plain how much he admired the Highland way of life that was being destroyed in his own lifetime. But when he wrote about social change, and speculated about its causes and effects, he drew his examples from ancient Greece and Rome, or the Red Indians of North America or almost anywhere but Scotland. The same is true of most of his fellow literati. Perhaps the reality of the Scottish situation after the Union and Culloden was so painful that they had to disguise their thought in generalities.

Certainly, there were many other contributory factors. Everywhere in Europe education was still preoccupied with Latin, and to a lesser extent with Greek. It was natural to look to Greece and Rome because their literature and history were more familiar to the educated than those of their own time and country. Sweeping generality was the fashion of the age. There were strong pressures on conformity with the ruling establishment because of their monopoly of patronage. The weight of the London market was already making itself felt. Both Hume and Smith found their publisher there, even if he was Scottish.

Also, there was another attitude which was more openly acknowledged in the second half of the eighteenth century than at any time before or since. Certain people in certain moods felt that they should make the best of a bad job and accept the political implications of the Union by resigning themselves to assimilation. It was a mood, especially acute after Culloden, of let us forget the past and try to be English. No doubt, there have been Scots then and subsequently who have followed this policy in practice, if not always in theory. They have always been a minority, although sometimes an influential one. They have remained a minority partly because of the resilience of the Scottish sense of identity and partly because of the attitude of the English themselves. There is a well-known letter in which David Hume (who was British Chargé d'Affaires in Paris at the time) replies to a suggestion of this sort. "Can you seriously talk of my continuing an Englishman? Am I, or are you, an Englishman? Will they allow us to be so? Do they not treat with Derision our Pretensions to that Name, and with Hatred our just Pretensions to surpass and to govern them?"[16]

Hume was more than half serious in talking about these pretensions. His letters are full of condemnation of the people whom he called "the Barbarians who inhabit the Banks of the Thames". "John Bull's predjudices are ridiculous", he remarked, "as his Insolence is intolerable". He wrote to Edward Gibbon to express polite surprise that an Englishman in that age could write a book of the quality of his *Decline and Fall of the Roman Empire*. The most frequently quoted passage of all from his letters is one where he salutes the achievements of the Scottish Enlightenment: "Really it is admirable how many Men of Genius this country produces at present. Is it not strange that, at a time when we have lost our Princes, our Parliaments, our independent Government, even the Presence of our chief Nobility, are unhappy in our Accent and Pronunciation, speak a very corrupt Dialect of the Tongue which we make use of; is it not strange, I say, that, in these Circumstances, we shou'd really be the People most distinguis'd for Literature in Europe?"[17] Adam Smith takes a similar position in his explanation of the reasons for the superiority of the Scottish Universities over the English.[18] There is a significant remark in Adam Ferguson's *Essay on the History of Civil Society*. The whole book is an argument in favour of the social advantages of life in a community, and he says: "We need not enlarge our communities, in order to enjoy these advantages. We frequently obtain them in the most remarkable degree, where nations remain independent, and are of small extent".[19] Whatever the reason for the flight of the Scottish Enlightenment literati into generality, it was not due to an inferiority complex or a lack of concern for the interest, standing and reputation of Scotland.

It remains true that the literati in most of their public utterances moved in a disembodied world of pure intellect. One of the first to criticise them for this was John Gibson Lockhart in his book *Peter's Letters to His Kinsfolk*, published in 1819. He discusses the whole question in a letter about a visit to Walter Scott at Abbotsford. The literati of the previous century, he says, had displayed a force of intellect as applied to matters of reasoning, but had largely neglected both feeling and the resources of Scottish history and literature. "The folly of slighting and concealing what remains concealed within herself, is one of the worst and most pernicious that can beset a country, in the situation wherein Scotland stands." Scott, he added, was the great genius who had shown Scotland "her own national character as a mine of intellectual wealth, which remains in a great measure unexplored".[20]

No one who reads much of Scott can fail to see that one of the mainsprings of his being was a deep concern about the erosion of the Scottish identity and a determination to resist it by drawing on the resources of Scottish history and literature. You can see it in the Introduction to his first substantial work, *The Minstrelsy of the Scottish Border* (1802):

> "By such efforts, feeble as they are, I may contribute something to the history of my native country, the peculiar features of whose manners and character are daily melting and dissolving into those of her sister and ally. And, trivial as may appear such an offering to the Manes of a Kingdom, once proud and independent, I hang it upon her altar with a mixture of feeling which I shall not attempt to describe."

"There is no mistaking" as Edwin Muir said, "the emotion in these words."[21] You can see it again in an episode, which Lockhart recounts in his *Life*, after a meeting of the Faculty of Advocates in Edinburgh in 1806. They had been discussing proposals to bring the administration of justice in Scotland closer to English practice. Lockhart tells us that Scott opposed them with "a flow and energy of eloquence for which those who knew him best had been quite unprepared". He continues:

> "When the meeting broke up, he walked across the Mound on his way to Castle Street, between Mr Jeffrey and another of his reforming friends, who complimented him on the rhetorical powers he had been displaying, and would willingly have treated the subject-matter of the discussion playfully. But his feeling had been moved to an extent far beyond their apprehension: he exclaimed, "No, no — 'tis no laughing matter; little by little, whatever your wishes may be, you will destroy and undermine, until nothing of what makes Scotland Scotland shall remain." And so saying, he turned round to conceal his agitation — but not until Mr Jeffrey saw tears gushing down his cheek — resting his head until he recovered himself on the wall of the Mound. Seldom, if ever, in his more advanced age, did any feelings obtain such mastery."[22]

These examples are from the beginning of Scott's career. The fullest statement of his feelings and opinions on these matters appeared towards the end of it in *The Letters of Malachi Malagrowther* of 1826. "I will sleep quieter in my grave," he told James Ballantyne, "for having so fair an opportunity of speaking my mind."[23] These Letters make a powerful case for the ideas that diversity is preferable to uniformity and centralisation; that Scottish characteristics are valuable for their own sake and should not be abandoned without good reason; that government should be responsive to local needs and wishes; that the overburdened government machine in London should refrain from interference in Scottish affairs.[24]

"There has been in England a gradual and progressive system of assuming the management of affairs entirely and exclusively proper to Scotland, as if we were totally unworthy of having the management of our own concerns."[25] Scott's position on this matter is very close to views which are widely held in Scotland today; we have still not found a remedy to the problem which disturbed him so deeply. MacDiarmid has pointed out that the line of Scott's thought "leads naturally on to the separatist position."[26] Indeed, when it comes to the question of Scotland, there is much in common between Scott, the professed Tory, and MacDiarmid, the professed Communist.

One might ask why this issue came to a head more than a hundred years after the Union. Scott's answer, and modern scholarship has confirmed that he was right, is that English interference began seriously only in the early nineteenth century. Before that, Scotland had been left to sink or swim by her own devices, with the disastrous exception of the suppression of the Highlands after the '45. When James Stuart Mackenzie was appointed in 1761 as the Minister responsible for Scotland, he was surprised to find no papers in his office and no sign that any business was being carried on.[27] Of course, at that time, and for long afterwards, the role of government was very limited. Education and such social services as existed were the concern not of the State, but of the Kirk and the burghs. The Union had left the Scottish legal system, the church and local government intact. They continued to function on their separate ways, although deprived of a Parliament to explore abuses and seek reforms. In Scott's words, Scotland had been left "under the guardianship of her own institutions, to win her silent way to national wealth and consequence. . . But neglected as she was, and perhaps *because* she was neglected, Scotland, reckoning her progress during the space from the close of the American war to the present day, has increased her prosperity in a ratio more than five times greater than that of her more fortunate and richer sister. She is now worth the attention of the learned faculty, and God knows she has plenty of it. . . . A spirit of proselytism has of late shown itself in England for extending the benefits of their system, in all its strength and weakness, to a country, which has been hitherto flourishing and contented under its own. They adopted the conclusion, that all English enactments are right; but the system of municipal law in Scotland is not English, therefore it is wrong."[28]

III. *The Nineteenth Century Decline*

Scotland in the early nineteenth century, when the Elephant began to assert itself, was "flourishing and contented" in more than a material sense. Her universities were still a major source of stimulation and new ideas for the whole world. The ministers of the Kirk had produced in the *Statistical Account* the first attempt anywhere to study conditions of a country in depth as a rational basis for future policy, even if Scotland had no parliament to give legislative effect to the ideas. Literature was more flourishing in Scotland than almost anywhere else. Scott was the dominant figure internationally, but he was not alone. Both Galt and Hogg were innovative but rooted in the Scottish tradition. *Blackwood's Magazine* and the *Edinburgh Review* were among the most influential periodicals in the world. The Edinburgh of the time was described by John Buchan in these words:

> "Many of the great academic figures had gone, but Dugald Stewart and John Playfair were alive; there was a national school of science and philosophy as well of letters, and there were scholarly country gentlemen, like Clerk of Eldin and Sir William

Forbes, to make a bridge between learning and
society. Edinburgh was a true capital, a clearing
house for the world's culture and a jealous repository
of Scottish tradition."[29]

Lord Cockburn, the most perceptive observer of the contemporary scene, described this period as "the last purely
Scotch age that Scotland was destined to see". "According to
the modern rate of travelling," he continued (he was writing
in 1852), "the capitals of Scotland and of England were then
about 2400 miles asunder. Edinburgh was still more distant
in its style and habits. It had then its own independent tastes,
and ideas, and pursuits."[30]

Already by 1852, Cockburn remarked on a sudden and
drastic change. The whole country had begun to be "absorbed
in the ocean of London." Edinburgh, to some extent, resis-
ted. "This city has advantages, including its being the capital
of Scotland, its old reputation, and its external beauties,
which have enabled it, in a certain degree, to resist the
centralising tendency, and have hitherto always supplied it
with a succession of eminent men. But, now that London is at
our door, how precarious is our hold of them, and how many
have we lost."[31] In his *Journal*, some twenty years earlier,
Scott had already remarked on the beginning of the same
process: "In London, there is a rapid increase of business and
its opportunities. Thus London licks the butter off our bread,
by opening a better market for ambition. Were it not for the
difference of the religion and laws, poor Scotland could
hardly keep a man that is worth having."[32] "Triumphant and
eclipsing England", wrote Lockhart, "like an immense magnet, absolutely draws the needles from the smaller ones."[33]

We might take Carlyle's departure for London in 1834 as
the symbolic date of this abrupt and astonishing loss of
self-confidence and achievement. For about 100 years Scotland, and Edinburgh in particular, had been in a ferment of

artistic and intellectual activity. It was a veritable renaissance which had profound effects on the evolution of the modern world. Both in its sources and its consequences it was international, but it was sustained by Scottish tradition and it was not dominated by any one external influence. A generation earlier, it would have been natural for Carlyle to stay in Scotland and participate in the intellectual excitement. By 1834, the interference of London in Scottish affairs, aided by the improved communications with railways and steamships, made it equally natural for him and countless others to succumb to the pull of the "immense magnet." "The operation of the commercial principle which tempts all superiority to try its fortune in the greatest accessible market, is perhaps irresistible," wrote Cockburn, "but anything is surely to be lamented which annihilates local intellect, and degrades the provincial spheres which intellect and its consequences can alone adorn."[34] This is precisely what happened. Scott, writing in 1826, had described the English pressure as beginning in "the last fifteen or twenty years, and more especially the last ten."[35] Within two or three decades, the pull and the pressure (for it worked both ways) threatened to reduce Scotland to provincial mediocrity.

The effect was most obvious in literature, which is, I suppose, as good an indication as any of the cultural health of a society. After the brilliance of Scott, Galt and Hogg, all of whom died in the 1830s, there is a melancholy hiatus for the next fifty years. Scotland, which had shown the way at the beginning, failed to continue the development of the realistic novel which distinguished the literatures of England, France and Russia in the mid-nineteenth century. There was, to use a phrase of George Davie's, a sorry "failure of intellectual nerve."[36] William Power's explanation is that Scottish writers had "lost the native tradition, the literary sense of Scottishness. They floundered about in the English scheme of things, and never caught on to anything vital."[37] Gaelic poetry suffered a similar decline. The sensitivity, intelligence and virtuosity of the eighteenth century was followed by a collapse into triviality in the nineteenth. In one of his letters, Scott said: "If you *unscotch* us, you will make us damned mischievous Englishmen."[38] Not so much mischievous, perhaps, as inadequate and second-rate.

An even more astonishing, and, one might think, impertinent campaign of anglicisation was directed against the most successful of Scottish institutions, the universities. They were, after all, the powerhouse of new ideas and of trained minds which had made the Scottish Enlightenment. They were respected, admired and imitated throughout the civilised world, except perhaps in England with its customary attitude of complacent insularity. At the same period, the two universities in England itself were sunk in lethargy, "steeped in port and prejudice", as Edward Gibbon expressed it.[39] Yet, from early in the nineteenth century, there was a determined and ultimately largely successful campaign to subordinate the Scottish universities to English standards. This whole subject is the theme of George Davie's classic book, *The Democratic Intellect*, one of the most important written in Scotland in this century. It was, he wrote, "the tortuous, dark revolution whereby a nation noted educationally both for social mobility and for fixity of first principle gradually reconciled itself to an alien system in which principles traditionally did not matter and a rigid social immobilism was the accepted thing." The intention was "to prepare the way for the cultural subordination of Scotland to England parallel to its political subordination."[40] Significantly, the first move in this campaign was in 1826, the year in which Scott wrote *The Letters of Malachi Malagrowther.*

Shortly after the publication of George Davie's book in 1961, C. P. Snow, who wrote one of the enthusiastic reviews of it, made a speech in Edinburgh. He summed up the matter in these words:

"150 years ago Edinburgh had probably the best University in the world, with a deep and serious intellectual tradition, which still exists in this country. I could wish that Scottish education had remained a little more different from English rather than the reverse, because the Scots have always believed in democratic education and in the general-ised intellect in a way that my more empirical countrymen have never quite believed."[41]

Another distinguished Englishman, V. H. Galbraith, was for many years Professor of British History in Edinburgh. When he left in 1944, he drew conclusions from his experien-ces in Scotland: "I am perfectly sure that the future of Scotland lies in a tremendous development of its own affairs, and having the power to do that. No proposal with regard to education which comes up here from England is worth a damn to you."[42] Unfortunately, this was not the view which had prevailed during the previous hundred years.

A similar process applied to the schools, again in spite of their acknowledged achievement. As in the universities, the school system was distorted in the course of the nineteenth century by the imposition of incompatible English ideas. One of the qualities of Scottish education from the sixteenth century was its accessibility to the whole population without distinction of social class. Take, for example, the High School of Edinburgh, described by James Grant as "the most important in Scotland and intimately connected with the literature and progress of the Kingdom."[43] In a speech in 1825 Lord Brougham said this about it: "A school like the old High School of Edinburgh is invaluable, and for what is this so? It is because men of the highest and lowest rank of society send their children to be educated together."[44] Yet at about the time he was saying this, it was becoming increasingly common for the aristocracy and the more socially ambitious of the middle class to send their sons to the so-called public schools in England which were run on the opposite principle of social exclusivity. For those who wanted to compromise, or who could not afford Eton or the rest, a number of schools on the English model began to be established in Scotland, beginning with the Edinburgh Academy in 1824. Apart from the social implications, there was a fundamental divergence in intellectual approach because the English, or imitation-English, schools believed in early specialisation in place of the Scottish principle of a general, broadly based education. The effect of all of this was socially divisive and it tended to create an influential class whose education, and therefore attitudes and allegiance, were more English than Scottish. They were predisposed to form an internal lobby favourably inclined towards anglicisation.

Even so, it is puzzling that the country succumbed so easily when it had such solid achievement behind it and such a history of determined resistance. There were a number of reasons, some peculiar to the period and some which have persisted. In the first place, the assertion of English influence in the early nineteenth century was contemporary with the victory over Napoleon. It was the beginning of a period, which lasted about 100 years, when Britain (which means predominantly England) was the richest and most successful of World Powers. It was the zenith of the British Empire which coloured a large part of the map of the world in red. England was in a triumphant and assertive mood and more than usually difficult to resist. The Napoleonic Wars had direct effects on Scotland. They caused the Establishment, either reacting in panic or seizing an opportunity, to suppress radicalism and curb the free expression of political ideas. At the same time, they encouraged a spirit of British patriotism which tended to displace or conceal traditional Scottish attitudes.

The development of the Empire was to a disproportionate

extent the work of Scots who were active everywhere as explorers, administrators, engineers, soldiers, doctors, missionaries and teachers. This preoccupation with careers in the Empire strongly contributed to the distortion of Scottish education. When entrance examinations for the overseas services were introduced, they were based on the English educational system and the Scottish schools and universities had to adjust accordingly if their candidates were to have a fair chance. This helped to establish a habit of concentration on English history and literature to the exclusion of the Scottish which still persists, much to the detriment of Scottish self-knowledge and self-confidence. It may well be true, as Elizabeth Hay wrote recently, that "the Scots participated in the Empire as Scots. They did not feel it was England's Empire. . . They thought of themselves as Scottish first and then British."[45] Even so, the energy which the Scots expended in India, Canada, Australia, New Zealand and Africa was lost to Scotland. The one benefit, if it was a benefit, which the Union brought to Scotland was access to careers in the Empire while it lasted. In any case, it was benefit to individuals, not to Scotland as a whole. When this loss of population is added to the wholesale clearance of the Highlands and the emigration compelled by the neglect of Scotland itself, it amounts to a massive haemorrhage of talent, energy and skill. This has been on a scale which threatens the very survival of Scotland; but Scotland had no Parliament even to discuss the matter and no government to take action. The haemorrhage has continued. Writing in 1935, Edwin Muir drew the obvious conclusion:

> "Scotland is gradually being emptied of its population, its spirit, its wealth, industry, art, intellect, and innate character. . . . If a country exports its most enterprising spirits and best minds year after year, for fifty or a hundred or two hundred years,

some result will enevitably follow. . . . (Scotland is)
a country which is becoming lost to history."[46]

In the early nineteenth century the people of Scotland were
even more defenceless than they are today. Not only was there
no Scottish Parliament, but only an insignificant part of the
population had the right to vote for the small minority of
Scottish members in the British House. Parliamentary
Reform began in 1832, but it was not until the Third Reform
Act of 1884 that most adult men, but still no women, had
the vote. It was only then that there began to be any real
opportunity for the people at large to have any influence on
events. It is probably not coincidental that it was at about the
same time, as we shall see, that some restraint began to be
applied to the nineteenth century decline.

On the other hand, if Scotland had no Parliament, it did
have the long-established democratic structure of the Church
of Scotland, several centuries in advance of Parliament in
accepting the democratic ideal of equality. Although the
General Assembly did not have the political power of a
Legislature, the Church was a great cohesive force in Scottish
society. It had far more impact on the lives of the people than
the remote Government in London, especially as it was
largely responsible for the social services. In Scott's phrase, it
was one of the "institutions" which carried on the life of the
country after it was deprived of its Parliament in 1707. As it
happened, the Church was incapacitated by an internal crisis
precisely at the time when English interference began to
assert itself and at the same time as the existing social
structure was under strain because of the effects of the new
industrialisation. The crisis was a consequence of the imposition of the system of patronage on the Church by Parliament,
although this violated guarantees contained in the Union
settlement itself. By 1843, this led to the remarkable event of
the Disruption, when 450 ministers of the Church, more

than a third of the total, gave up their churches, homes and incomes for the sake of their conscience. It was, Cockburn wrote, "as extraordinary, and in its consequences will probably prove as permanent as any single transaction in the history of Scotland, the Union alone excepted. . . . It is one of the rarest occurrences in moral history. I know of no parallel to it."[47] Eventually the Church for the most part reunited, but it never regained the pivotal position which it had held in the life of the country before the Disruption. Nothing has, so far, taken its place. Scotland as never before was left, in Edwin Muir's phrase, with "no centre, no heart radiating a living influence."[48] It is a vacuum which in modern conditions only a Parliament can fill.

For all these reasons, Scotland was particularly vulnerable to anglicisation when the process began effectively in the early nineteenth century. The most systematic study of it so far has been one by an American sociologist, Michael Hechter, in his book *Internal Colonialism*, first published in 1975. He identifies three characteristics:

1. "A defining characteristic of imperial expansion is that the centre must disparage the indigenous culture of peripheral groups."

2. "One of the consequences of this denigration of indigenous culture is to undermine the native's will to resist the colonial regime."

(I might remark in passing that one of the commonest forms of this denigration is to describe anything Scottish as "parochial" or "narrowly Nationalist", and this is usually said by someone who is himself particularly parochial and chauvinist.)

3. "Political incorporation also had a decisive effect on the progress of anglicisation, which proceeded not only by government fiat, but through the voluntary assimilation of peripheral elites."[49]

The implications of Hechter's analysis is that this process, which also applied to Wales and Ireland, was the result of a deliberate and sustained government policy. At least as far as Scotland is concerned, I do not think that this is normally true. English policy in this respect has usually been unconscious, except in moments of panic, as in 1745 and the 1970s. It has been the result more of ignorance and indifference over Scottish interests and aspirations than of a conscious plan to thwart them. In R. L. Stevenson's words, "The egoism of the Englishman is self-contained. He does not seek to proselytise. He takes no interest in Scotland or the Scots, and, what is the unkindest cut of all, he does not care to justify his indifference."[50] The sheer elephantine weight of greater numbers and wealth, and a majority of about ten to one in Parliament, has applied itself without conscious effort. The assumption, as Scott said in the *Malachi* letters, has always been that what is English is right and what is not English is therefore wrong.

On the other hand, the efforts of those that Hechter calls the "peripheral elite," the internal anglicisers, have often been deliberate and even painstaking. In Hechter's words, "The conscious rationale behind anglicisation among the peripheral elite was to dissociate themselves as much as possible from the mass of their countrymen, who were so strongly deprecated by the English culture. Thus, they eagerly learned to speak English in the home, to emulate English manners and attitudes, to style their very lives on the English model. In effect, this was a voluntary renunciation of their national origins."[51] This is a phenomenon which began with a small minority as long ago as the Union of the Crowns in 1603. When the King and Court moved to London, the politically and socially ambitious inevitably followed and had to adopt English speech and fashions if they were to be found acceptable. After 1707, Scottish members of Parliament had to do the same to avoid the mockery of the House of Commons. Careers in government service had the same

effect. We have already noted the influence of this on the
Scottish educational system which in consequence itself tended to become an instrument of anglicisation. To this were
added in more recent times the forces of the London press
and, even more powerfully, of radio and television. By these
means, and once again largely unconsciously on their part,
generations of Scots have been brought up to regard English
traditions and habits of thought and expression as the norm
and to be left almost entirely in ignorance of their own. It is
easy to see why Muir felt that Scotland was "a country which
is becoming lost to history."

IV. *Does It Matter?*

Are we then an endangered species, about to become in fact,
as some people already regard us, no more than the inhabi-
tants of a region of England? If so, does it matter? Should we
perhaps yield to superior force and give up the struggle? I
think that the answer to all of these questions depends on
whether there is anything of value in the Scottish tradition
which is worth an effort to preserve.

There is first of all the consideration that diversity has a
value in itself and is to be preferred to uniformity, especially
when it is imposed by external circumstances. This is a
proposition to which most people would, I suppose, sub-
scribe. A world reduced to uniformity would not only be
dull, but also sterile; inventiveness and the arts would be
stifled. Most of us would, as it were, be thinking in translation and trying to adopt attitudes which are not natural to us.
Imitation is always likely to be inferior to the spontaneous.
As Scott said in the *Malachi* letters:

> "For God's sake, sir, let us remain as Nature made

us, Englishmen, Irishmen, and Scotchmen, with something like the impress of our several countries upon each! We would not become better subjects, or more valuable members of the common empire, if we all resembled each other like so many smooth shillings. Let us love and cherish each other's virtues — bear with each other's failings — be tender to each other's prejudices — be scrupulously regardful of each other's rights. Lastly, let us borrow each other's improvements, but never before they are needed and demanded. The degree of national diversity between different countries, is but an instance of that general variety which Nature seems to have adopted as a principle through all her works, as anxious, apparently, to avoid, as modern statesmen to enforce, anything like an approach to absolute uniformity."[52]

T. S. Eliot, consciously or unconsciously echoing Scott, argued, "it is to the advantage of England that the Welsh should be Welsh, the Scots Scots and the Irish Irish. . . . It is an essential part of my case, that if the other cultures of the British Isles were wholly superseded by English culture, English culture would disappear too."[53] And the principle, of course, has a much wider application than to the British Isles alone.

The world as a whole has never had more need to defend its diversity than today. The forces working towards a monotonous uniformity have never been stronger from the power of mass consumerism, mass advertising and mass entertainment. The rich diversity of human cultures is threatened by a stifling overlay of a meretricious appeal to the lowest common denominator. Pop music is its most obvious and appropriate symbol with its monotonous repetition and trite lyrics expressed in mock American speech, regardless of the natural language of the singer or his audience. It is in the interests of mankind as a whole that each of us should preserve our identity from the flood which threatens to engulf all of us. The Scottish struggle is part of a world struggle.

In Scotland we have had long experience of the consequences of the imposition through the schools and social pressures of external cultural standards. For over 200 years our schools have tried to suppress natural speech, Gaelic or Scots, and make their pupils ape the English. They have diverted attention from our own history, literature and achievement to those of England. The consequence has been a loss of articulacy, spontaneity and self-confidence. If a child is taught to be ashamed of his natural speech, he tends to lose all confidence in self expression. If he is made to believe that everything of importance happened somewhere else, he is led towards an inferiority complex and a feeling of hopelessness and despair. It is a recipe for an unhealthy society, conditioned to failure, where the only hope is the escape of emigration.

That anything like this should happen in Scotland is particularly remarkable and outrageous in view of the extraordinary record of Scottish achievement. In the words of an American, Harold Orel: "The record is rich, when seen as an entirety, almost unbelievably so. No nation of its size has contributed as much to world culture."[54] Another American, H. W. Thompson, in discussing the Scotland of the Enlightenment in the life time of Henry Mackenzie, concluded: "To discover comparable achievements by so small a nation in so short a time we should need to go back from the Age of Mackenzie to the Age of Pericles."[55] Yet another American, J. K. Galbraith, said that "the only serious rivals to the Scots were the Jews."[56] These comparisons are not exaggerated. "The peculiar history of the Scots," wrote Christopher Harvie, "has meant that, man for man, they have probably done more to create the modern world than any other nation."[57] Watt's improvements of the steam engine created the first Industrial Revolution. Clerk Maxwell's discoveries ushered in the new revolution of electronics. The modern approach to such diverse matters as history, economics, sociology, geology, chemistry, medicine and banking were all fundamentally affected by the Scottish Enlightenment. We have produced a notable literature in four languages, including much of the greatest poetry of the late Middle Ages. Our traditional song, poetry and dance are among the most vigorous to be found anywhere. Scots have made a remarkable contribution to many European countries as well as to those of the former British Empire all over the world. You would expect us all to agree with the judgement of the English historian, J. A. Froude: "No nation in Europe can look with more just pride on their past than the Scots, and no young Scotchman [and I would add woman, of course] ought to grow up in ignorance of what that past has been."[58] The anglicisation of our education has decreed otherwise. Ironically, at the same time, there is increasing appreciation of the Scottish contribution to our common civilisation in other countries from America to Japan.

It would be a particular loss of a component of human diversity if the Scottish approach to life were supplanted by the English because they are so fundamentally different, socially and intellectually. We share with the French, and perhaps this is the reason for the remarkable persistence of the spirit of the Auld Alliance, a fondness for first principles and an appreciation of precision and logic. The English distrust these things and make a virtue of acting by instinct without a rigorous, and perhaps inhibiting, intellectual analysis. The formidable English historian, H. T. Buckle, one of the great Victorians, made a deep study of this question as part of his preparation for his *History of Civilisation*. His conclusion was that there was:

> "An essential antagonism which still exists between the Scotch and English minds; an antagonism

extremely remarkable, when found among nations,
both of whom, besides being contiguous, and con-
stantly mixing together, speak the same language,
read the same books, belong to the same empire, and
possess the same interests, and yet are, in many
important respects, as different, as if there had never
been any means of their influencing each other, and
as if they had never had anything in common."[59]

It is not, of course, a question of the superiority of one
national tradition over another. All have their strengths and
weaknesses; but the more diverse they are, the more likely
they are to enrich our common civilisation with a wide range
of achievement and offer a choice of different possible solutions to our problems. It is an impoverishment of civilisation
as a whole, if a valuable national tradition is suppressed or
supplanted by another. At the same time, the cross-fertilisa-
tion of ideas and influence is a fruitful source of stimulation,
provided the recipient is free to take, in Scott's words, what is
"needed and demanded", and to reject what is not suitable for
his purposes. This is something which is quite different from
the stifling imposition by force or elephantine weight of
different standards, attitudes and values from one particular
source. The great medieval poetry of Scotland and the Scottish Enlightenment are examples of the benefits of wide
international influence. The collapse of confidence and
achievement after about 1830 is an example of the consequences of elephantine pressure.

Eric Linklater in his book, *The Lion and the Unicorn* of
1935, summed up the effects of the sustitution of English
culture for "that diversity of cultures with which, in earlier
times, Scotland had always been in contact":

"By reason of its association with England, Scotland
became insular. Its political frontier was broken
down and its mind was walled up. Geographical or

political enlargement, beyond certain limits, is nearly always accompanied by intellectual shrinkage."[60]

V. *Revival*

In *The Democratic Intellect* George Davie says that in the Scotland of the nineteenth century, "the old confident grip on the situation was noticeably slackening. Instead of the steady rhythm of independent institutional life, a new pattern emerged of alternation between catastrophe and renaissance, in which the distinctive national inheritance was more than once brought to the very brink of ruin only to be saved at the last minute by a sudden burst of reviving energy."[61] In the mid-nineteenth century, Scotland seemed about to decline into passive acceptance of provincial mediocrity, into what C. J. Watson has described as "the sense of weariness, of the absence of hope, and lacerating self-contempt which is a marked component in the psyche of colonised peoples."[62]

Even so, the decline was only in comparison to the generation before. There was strong resilience in the Scottish spirit in spite of the conformity on the surface. In Scotland, oral and traditional literature has always nourished and been nourished by literature of the more formal kind, as in the revival introduced by Watson and Ramsay in the eighteenth century. These traditions remained vigorously alive. In the mid-century, J. F. Campbell collected four volumes of Gaelic traditional stories. Towards the end of the century, Gavin Greig and the Rev. James Duncan found about 3,000 Scots songs alive in folk tradition in Buchan alone. William MacTaggart was painting from about the middle of the century. Brewster, Kelvin and Clerk Maxwell continued the scientific traditions of the Enlightenment, although they were no longer sustained by the "independent institutional life" which had encouraged the achievements of the previous century.

The first coherent "burst of reviving energy" came in the 1880s and 1890s. In this, as subsequently, political developments and the formation of new institutions coincided with a resurgence of literature and the other arts. It seems that a quickening of one aspect of Scottish life stimulates the others. In the 1880s, for instance, the Scottish Home Rule Association was formed and the conference of the Scottish Liberal Party adopted for the first time the policy of Home Rule for Scotland. Parliament passed an Act to re-establish the office of Secretary of State. The National Portrait Gallery, the Scottish Text Society and the Scottish History Society were formed. Stevenson wrote *Kidnapped* and *The Master of Ballantrae*. By 1895, Sir Patrick Geddes was able to write in his periodical, *Evergreen*, of a Scots Renaissance, long before the term was applied to the movement associated with Hugh MacDiarmid. Geddes was himself a leader in this revival, devoted to the cause of escaping from the "intellectual thraldom of London" and restoring the old sympathies between Scotland and the Continent.[63] In the same spirit, he tried to found a College des Ecossais in Montpellier as a revival of the Scots College in Paris, established in 1326 as the first Scottish institution of higher learning.

The First World War intervened, with the destructive effects on Scottish communities chronicled by Lewis Grassic Gibbon in *Sunset Song*. Like the Napoleonic Wars, it diverted attention away from Scotland's own concerns. On the other hand, it purported to be a war fought for the right of self-determination and it did lead to the restoration of several small nations to the map of Europe. These ideas contributed to second wave of "reviving energy" in the 1920s and 30s. This is associated particularly with Hugh MacDiarmid who campaigned throughout his life for Scottish independence and for a revival, not only of Scots and Gaelic, but of Scottish culture in the widest sense, far-ranging both in intellectual content and in its international ramifications. His work resumes and restates many of the constant themes of Scottish writing. In resisting anglicisation, he was echoing Scott; in returning to Dunbar for inspiration and example, he was following the lead of Ramsay; in extending the use of Scots, he was building on the foundation of Fergusson and Burns; in responding to the latest tendencies in international thought, and regarding all knowledge as an interlocking whole, he was in the tradition of the Scottish Enlightenment; in his radical politics he was extending a tradition that goes back through MacLean, Muir of Huntershill, the Covenanters, the Reformation and George Buchanan to the Declaration of Arbroath. "To MacDiarmid," wrote Tom Scott, "the English Ascendancy was a historical iniquity with no right but might behind it, and to be overthrown by all good men and true."[64]

Once again, literary, political and institutional developments moved forward together. MacDiarmid published *A Drunk Man Looks at the Thistle* in 1926. He became the centre of a very lively literary life, with poets, novelists and dramatists like Sydney Goodsir Smith, Robert Garioch, Sorley MacLean, George Campbell Hay, Neil Gunn, Lewis Grassic Gibbon, Eric Linklater, Robert Kemp, Robert Maclellan and many others. The National Library of Scotland was established in 1925 on the basis of the Advocates Library, founded in 1682. (Like the National Portrait Gallery, it was made possible by private generosity). In 1936, the Saltire Society was formed to "work for a revival of the intellectual and artistic life of Scotland such as we experienced in the eighteenth century." The Scottish National Party was founded in 1934 by the fusion of two older parties. In 1939, the Government moved Departments concerned with Scotland from London to Edinburgh.

Again, a World War deferred expectations and scattered

the men involved in the new atmosphere of intellectual vitality. However, during the War itself, MacDiarmid and the others continued to write and plan and work for the future. Tom Johnston as Secretary of State gave an impetus to the search for Scottish solutions to Scottish problems. Scottish Convention began a campaign which led in 1949 to the collection of some two million signatures to a Covenant demanding a Scottish Parliament. In the immediate post-war period, both the political and the intellectual movements gathered momentum. The first Edinburgh International Festival was held in 1947. In the same year, the Scottish Arts Council became largely autonomous (although constitutionally still a part of the Arts Council of Great Britain). Since then it has been a valuable channel of public subsidy to the arts, and has contributed substantially to the revival of Scottish publishing and to the emergence of a diversity of literary magazines. Scottish historical scholarship in particular has acquired new vitality and challenged many accepted ideas of the Scottish past. The electoral successes of the SNP in the 1960s and 70s attracted attention as never before to Scottish issues. All political parties committed themselves to a measure of Scottish self-government. When the Scotland Act was put to the people in the Referendum of 1979, however, the Conservative Party campaigned for a "No" vote with the promise that they would introduce an improved measure with stronger powers. They then used the small "Yes" majority as a justification for taking no further action.

The optimism and self-confidence generated by the hopes of constitutional advance in the 1970s led to a marked quickening of the national life. There was an injection of new spirit into the Scottish theatre and a strong increase in the writing and publication of serious Scottish books. Planning for a revitalised Scotland was very active. The Saltire Society, for example, held a conference in 1977 to consider the policies necessary in an autonomous Scotland for the encouragement of artistic and intellectual life. The conference decided to consult all organisations concerned with these matters with a view to the formation of a combined think-tank. This, the Advisory Council for the Arts in Scotland, was established after wide consultation in 1981, two years after the Referendum.

This continuation of effort in spite of the setback was not untypical. There is no doubt that the muted "Yes" majority in the Referendum, and the confusion of the issues by the disingenuousness of the "No" campaign, brought with it a mood of humiliation and resignation. At the same time, the forward momentum was not entirely lost, even if much of it went below the surface. All political parties, with the present exception of the Conservatives, are more fully committed than ever to self-government, and these parties had more than 70% of the Scottish vote in the last two general elections. The Campaign for a Scottish Assembly has been active in promoting co-operation between the parties and in drawing up detailed plans for a Constitutional Convention. Constitutional advance now seems only a matter of time, but there is not much time left before it is too late.

This consideration of contemporary politics is unavoidable because it is central to the issue. In Donald Dewar's words, "There is a real connection between political power and the survival of a culture."[65] The close association which we have noted between political and cultural confidence and activity is not accidental. They have advanced together and declined together. Scotland is threatened with extinction as an active, creative component of European civilisation because of the vacuum at its heart, the absence of any focus for the national life and the denial of responsibility for its own affairs. "I believe"said Eric Linklater, "people degenerate when they lose control of their own affairs, and as a corollary that resumption of control may induce regeneration. To any nation the essential vitamin is responsibility."[66]

Scotland is now poised for a new surge of political and cultural advance. It has been a slow process, but each of the surges during the last 100 years has left us a little further up the beach. We are equipped as never before with the tools for an intelligent understanding of our position, both in the results of the new historical scholarship and in such reference works as the *Companions* of David Daiches, Derek Thomson and Trevor Royle. W. L. Lorimer's *Translation of the New Testament* has given new force to Scottish prose. *The Concise Scots Dictionary* has made widely available the great resources of *The Scottish National Dictionary* and the *Dictionary of the Older Scottish Tongue.* The Report in 1985 of the Consultative Committee on the Curriculum was a positive revolution in the thought of Scottish educationalists. Their recommendation that "the Scottish dimension, Scottish language, literature, geography and history are not frills, but should be central to the education of the children who attend Scottish schools"[67] may seem self-evident but it is far from the practice which has prevailed up to the present. At the same time, there has probably never been a stronger political consensus on the need for constitutional change. As I write, the latest opinion poll on the subject shows a majority in favour of an independent Parliament. That is what we need. Any degree of self-government would be beneficial; but for Scotland to be free to develop and play its full part in Europe as in the past, it needs as much independence as Luxembourg or Denmark or any other member of the EEC.

Can we then be optimistic? Are we to be saved at the eleventh hour by another "burst of reviving energy"? Only, I think, if we all make a determined effort. All the positive forces which I have mentioned are opposed, if largely unconsciously, by the forces of assimilation and they have the weight of superior numbers and wealth on their side. Our minds are flooded daily by television programmes and very few of them originate in Scotland. To the activities of the internal anglicisers, who are always with us, are added an increasing number of immigrants who actually are English. This is a new phenomenon on anything like the present scale. We welcome them, as is proper, with our traditional hospitality. Many of them take trouble to learn about us and bring with them qualities of real value. Others live in a cocoon of deliberate and complacent ignorance of the society that surrounds them. This would not matter very much, except that many of them occupy key positions in our institutions, even in those which are supposed to be the custodians of our traditions and values. This is prevalent not only in Government but in the universities, the theatre and even in local arts festivals where there is often no Scottish element at all. We are sometimes left feeling like strangers in our own country who are gradually being displaced by a colonial regime. It was such a thought as this that led James Campbell to say of the Clearances in his book, *Invisible Country* in 1984: "Throughout the entire country there is the sense that what took place in the Highlands during the earlier part of last century is a clue to what has happened to modern Scotland."[68]

One of the founding members of the Saltire Society, Andrew Dewar Gibb, in considering the consequences of the elephantine pressures, concluded: "Thus have closer ties with England resulted in the debasement, if not the total destruction, of a great national possession,"[69] When you consider the facts, this is a conclusion which it is difficult to avoid. As I have said, I do not think that this effect has been deliberate or malevolent, at least since the suppression of the Highlands; but it is inherent in the present constitutional position. We want to have friendly and productive relationships with all countries, and certainly with our nearest neighbour. Not the least of the reasons why we urgently need a constitutional change is that otherwise an equitable and fair relationship with England is impossible.

REFERENCES

1. Henry Thomas Buckle *On Scotland and the Scotch Intellect* (Part of his *History of Civilisation in England* 1857 and 1861) ed. H. J. Hanham (Chicago 1970) p.31.

2. James Anthony Froude *History of England from the Fall of Wolsey to the Defeat of the Spanish Armada* (London 1873) Vol. IV p.5.

3. *The Declaration of Arbroath* ed. Sir James Fergusson (Edinburgh 1970) p.9.

4. Robert Burns in a letter to Dr John Moore of 2 Aug. 1787 in *The Letters of Robert Burns* ed. J. De Lancey Ferguson (Oxford 1931) Vol. I p.106.

5. John Hill Burton *The Scot Abroad* (Edinburgh 1881) pp.364-5.

6. Dugald Stewart *Collected Works* ed. Sir William Hamilton (Edinburgh 1884) Vol. I p.551.

7. Francis Jeffrey in his review of Scott's *Marmion* in the *Edinburgh Review* of April 1808 (Vol. XII).

8. John Grierson 'The Salt of the Earth' in *John Grierson's Scotland* ed. Forsyth Hardy (Edinburgh 1979) p.33.

9. T. B. Macaulay *History of England* (London 1858) Vol. IV pp.782-3.

10. Sir Walter Scott *Rob Roy* Chapter 20.

11. John MacQueen *Progress and Poetry: The Enlightenment and Scottish Literature* (Edinburgh 1982) p.5.

12. Quoted in R. L. Mackie *King James IV of Scotland* (Edinburgh 1958) p.93.

13. This is discussed in my *1707: The Union of Scotland and England* (Edinburgh 1979), especially chapter 7.

14. Edward Topham *Letters from Edinburgh 1774-5* (London 1776, Facsimile Edition, Edinburgh 1971) p.55.

15.   John Ramsay of Ochtertyre *Scotland and Scotsmen in the Eighteenth Century* ed. A. A. Allardyce (Edinburgh and London 1888) Vol. I p.9.

16.   David Hume in a letter to Gilbert Elliot of Minto of 22 Sept. 1764 in *The Letters of David Hume* ed. J. Y. T. Greig (Oxford 1932) Vol. I.

17.   Ibid. Vol. I p.436, p.121, Vol. II pp.309-10, Vol. I p.255.

18.   Adam Smith *The Wealth of Nations* (1776) Book V, Chapters I and II. Everyman's Library Edition (London 1971) Vol. II pp. 247 and 291 to 294.

19.   Adam Ferguson *An Essay on the History of Civil Society* (1767) ed. Duncan Forbes (Edinburgh 1966) p.59.

20.   John Gibson Lockhart *Peter's Letters to his Kinsfolk* (Edinburgh 1819) Vol. II, Letter LV p.359.

21.   Edwin Muir *Scott and Scotland: The Predicament of the Scottish Writer* (London 1936) p.137.

22.   John Gibson Lockhart *Memoirs of Sir Walter Scott* (1837-8) Chapter XV.

23.   Sir Walter Scott in a letter to James Ballantyne of 26-27 Feb. 1826 in *The Letters of Sir Walter Scott* ed. H. J. C. Grierson (London 1932-37) Vol. IX p.437.

24.   Sir Walter Scott *The Letters of Malachi Malagrowther* (1826) ed. P. H. Scott (Edinburgh 1981). See also my *Walter Scott and Scotland* (Edinburgh 1981), especially chapter 7.

25.   Ibid p.136.

26.   Hugh MacDiarmid *Lucky Poet: A Self-study in Literature and Political Ideas*. (London 1943) p.203.

27.   Alexander Murdoch *The People Above: Politics and Administration in Mid-Eighteenth Century Scotland* (Edinburgh 1980) p.106.

28.   As 24, pp.10 and 9.

29.   John Buchan *Sir Walter Scott* (London 1932). Edition of 1961. pp.209-10.

30.   Henry Cockburn *Life of Francis Jeffrey*. Edition of 1872 (Edinburgh) pp.151 and 153.

31. Ibid. p.154.

32. Sir Walter Scott *Journal*. Entry for 24 March 1829. Edition of 1891 (Edinburgh) p.670.

33. As 20, p.356.

34. As 30, p.153.

35. As 24, p.4.

36. George Elder Davie *The Democratic Intellect: Scotland and Her Universities in the Nineteenth Century* (Edinburgh 1961) p.337.

37. William Power *My Scotland* (Edinburgh 1934) p.296.

38. Sir Walter Scott in a letter to J. W. Croker of 19 March 1826. As 23, Vol. IX p.472.

39. Edward Gibbon *Autobiography* Everyman's Library Edition. (London 1932) p.81.

40. As 36, pp.106 and 58.

41. C. P. Snow in a speech in Edinburgh to the International Federation of Library Associations on 4 Sept. 1961. (*The Scotsman* of 5 Sept. 1961).

42. V. H. Galbraith in a speech to the Historical Association of Scotland on 1 March 1944 (*The Scotsman* of 2 March 1944).

43. James Grant *Old and New Edinburgh* (London 1880) p.110.

44. Henry Brougham in a speech in Edinburgh on 5 April 1825. (*The Scotsman* of 6 April 1825).

45. Elizabeth Hay *Sambo Sahib* (Edinburgh 1981) p.111.

46. Edwin Muir *Scottish Journey* (1935). Edition of 1979 (Edinburgh) pp.3 and 4.

47. Henry Cockburn *Journal* (Edinburgh 1874) Vol. II pp.31-2.

48. As 21, p.144.

49. Michael Hechter *Internal Colonialism: The Celtic Fringe in British National Development* (London 1975) pp.64, 73, 80, 81.

50. R. L. Stevenson: "The Foreigner at Home" in *Memories and Portraits* (1887).

51. As 49, p.117.

52. As 24, p.143.

53. T. S. Eliot *Notes Towards the Definition of Culture* (London 1948) p.57.

54. Harold Orel *The Scottish World: History and Culture of Scotland* (London 1981) p.12.

55. H. W. Thompson *Henry Mackenzie: A Scottish Man of Feeling* (London and New York 1931) p.1.

56. J. K. Galbraith in a BBC television programme in 1977.

57. Christopher Harvie *Scotland and Nationalism: Scottish Society and Politics. 1707-1977.* (London 1977) p.18.

58. J. A. Froude quoted by Professor Gordon Donaldson in his Inaugural Lecture in the University of Edinburgh, 1964.

59. As 1, p.395.

60. Eric Linklater *The Lion and the Unicorn* (London 1935) p.130.

61. As 36, p.xvi.

62. C. J. Watson in *Literature of the North* ed. David Hewitt and Michael Spiller (Aberdeen 1983) p.140.

63. Philip Mairet *Pioneer of Sociology: The Life and Letters of Patrick Geddes* (London 1957) p.68.

64. Tom Scott in his Introduction to *The Penguin Book of Scottish Verse* (Harmondsworth 1970) p.50.

65. Donald Dewar in *The Scottish Debate* ed. Neil MacCormick (Oxford 1970) p.77.

66. As 60 p.26-7.

67. *Scottish Resources in Schools*, a Discussion Paper published by the Dundee College of Education for the Consultative Committee on the Curriculum, 1985.

68. James Campbell *Invisible Country: A Journey Through Scotland.* (London 1984) p.83.

69. Andrew Dewar Gibb *Scotland Resurgent* (Stirling 1950) p.203.